To

_____

From

_____

Date

_____

A good father is one of the most unsung, unpraised, unnoticed, and yet one of the most valuable assets in our society.
—Billy Graham

A Gift Book for Dads and Those Who Wish to Celebrate Them

What If There Were No Dads?

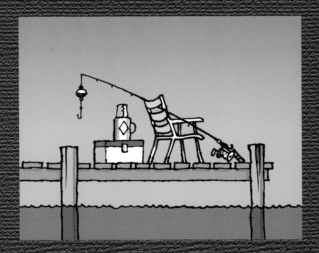

Caron Chandler Loveless
Illustrations by Dennis Hill

HOWARD BOOKS
A DIVISION OF SIMON & SCHUSTER
New York   London   Toronto   Sydney

We'd try not to panic
or start to feel bad.
We'd ask, "Where would we go
if we were a dad?"

We'd check our garages, look under the car,
Thinking our dads really never go far.

When dads were not there,
we would all scratch our heads.
Then just for good measure,
check under our beds.

We'd head to that spot
at the lake where dads fish,
With their pole and some bait
and a giant fish wish.

But if it was true, dads had vanished from sight,
We'd shake in our boots, our faces ghost white.

We'd pout on the
playground and
not do a thing.
With daddies gone missing,
well, who'd push the swing?

Forget about camping or tracking a bear,
Who'd build a warm fire if daddies weren't there?

And breakfast on weekends would be no more fun.
No dad yelling, "Hurry! The pancakes are done!"

Then in the night when we heard a strange sound
Who'd turn on the light, have a good look around?

No tickling, no teasing, no rolls on the ground,
Horseplay would halt if no dads were around.

Who'd drive us cross-country without a pit stop?
Then make us hike mountains clear up to the top?

And there'd be no dancing on Daddy's big feet,
No twirling or twisting to that rock and roll beat.

Who would bring up the car
when it's pouring down rain,
Just to keep us all dry
with no need to complain?

Who would point to the sky
and name every star,
Then say right out loud
just how special we are?

When parades come to town and kids couldn't see,
Who'd lift them on shoulders or climb up a tree?

Who'd shovel snow when blizzards blow through,
When temperatures reach ten degrees minus two?

Forget playing games like checkers or chess.
There'd be no charades without fathers to guess.

Who would chop wood,

paint the fence,

wash the cars?

Yikes! All of Dad's chores would now become ours!

To master a sport might
become extra hard
Without golf or football
or catch in the yard.

To plays and recitals no one would bring flowers
Or patiently wait while we practiced for hours.

And help with math homework—
well, let's not go there
Without dads to coach us we'd just sit and stare.

Without father wisdom, just where would kids be?
The right path to take would be harder to see.

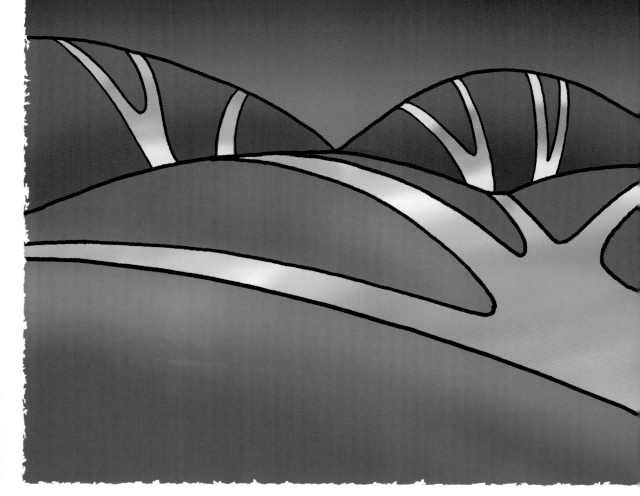

So let it be known that if I get a choice
I'd shout, "Need you, Dad!" at the top of my voice.

Your value to me is triple a ton.

The main man in my life, yes, you are the one.

A day without you, Dad, I truly must say,

That just cannot happen,

Absolutely

Fathers, don't exasperate your children
by coming down hard on them.
Take them by the hand and lead them
in the way of the Master.
—Ephesians 6:4 (The Message)

Dad, I couldn't live without you because:

_____

_____

_____

_____

_____

_____

_____

_____

_____

_____

_____

Our purpose at Howard Books is to:
• *Increase faith* in the hearts of growing Christians
• *Inspire holiness* in the lives of believers
• *Instill hope* in the hearts of struggling people everywhere
Because He's coming again!

Published by Howard Books, a division of Simon & Schuster, Inc.
1230 Avenue of the Americas, New York, NY 10020
www.howardpublishing.com

What If There Were No Dads? © 2009 by Caron Chandler Loveless

ISBN-13: 978-1-4165-5199-7
ISBN-10:   1-4165-5199-9

10 9 8 7 6 5 4 3 2 1

HOWARD and colophon are registered trademarks of Simon & Schuster, Inc.

Manufactured in China

For information regarding special discounts for bulk purchases, please contact: Simon & Schuster Special Sales at 1-800-456-6798 or business@simonandschuster.com.

Edited by Chrys Howard
Cover design by Stephanie D. Walker
Interior design by Dennis Hill and Stephanie D. Walker
Illustrations by Dennis Hill